Detroit Pistons Epic History

Epic History

Published by Epic History, 2024.

While every precaution has been taken in the preparation of this book, the publisher assumes no responsibility for errors or omissions, or for damages resulting from the use of the information contained herein.

DETROIT PISTONS EPIC HISTORY

First edition. February 29, 2024.

Copyright © 2024 Epic History.

ISBN: 979-8224757039

Written by Epic History.

Also by Epic History

New Jersey Devils Epic History
Detroit Red Wings Epic History
Dallas Mavericks Epic History
Denver Nuggets Epic History
Detroit Pistons Epic History
Golden State Warriors Epic History
Los Angeles Lakers Epic History

Table of Contents

Detroit Pistons Epic History

The Detroit Pistons: A Look into Their Colorful History

1. Introduction to the Detroit Pistons

The Detroit Pistons are a professional basketball team based in Detroit, Michigan. They are members of the National Basketball Association (NBA) and began play in the 1945-1946 season. Over the years, the Pistons have had their fair share of ups and downs, but they have always remained a beloved and iconic part of the city of Detroit. In this article, we will take a look at the colorful history of the Detroit Pistons, from their early years to their recent successes and challenges.

2. Early Years of the Detroit Pistons

The early years of the Detroit Pistons were marked with a strong commitment to defense and physical play, which helped establish them as one of the top teams in the NBA during the 1950s and 1960s. Under the leadership of legendary coach Red Auerbach, the team made its first appearance in the NBA Finals in 1957, where they faced off against the Boston Celtics. Although they ultimately fell short in their quest for a championship, the Pistons remained competitive throughout the decade, highlighted by a run to the NBA Finals again in 1960. In the following years, the team struggled to find success on the court, but remained a beloved fixture in the Detroit community.

3. Pistons' Success in the 1980s

During the 1980s, the Detroit Pistons experienced unprecedented success on the court. Led by head coach Chuck Daly and a group of talented players including Isiah Thomas, Joe Dumars, and Dennis Rodman, the team became known as the "Bad Boys" due to their aggressive and physical playing style. In the 1987-88 season, the Pistons won an impressive 50 games and went all the way to the NBA Finals where they faced off against the Los Angeles Lakers. Despite losing the series, the Pistons had proven themselves as a force to be reckoned with in the league. Over the next few years, the team continued to dominate with five consecutive trips to the NBA Finals from 1988 to 1993.

4. The Bad Boys Era

During the late 1980s and early 1990s, the Detroit Pistons were known as the "Bad Boys." This era was marked by physical play, tough defense, and a fearless attitude on the court. Led by players like Isiah Thomas, Joe Dumars, and Dennis Rodman, the Pistons became one of the most dominant teams in the NBA during this time. They made it to the NBA Finals three times in a row from 1988 to 1991, winning back-to-back championships in 1989 and 1990. The Bad Boys Era was a testament to the power of teamwork, toughness, and determination. It remains a cherished part of Detroit Pistons history and a source of pride for fans of the team.

5. Challenges and Rebuilding Efforts

After experiencing success in the 1980s as one of the "Bad Boys" of the NBA, the Detroit Pistons faced several challenges in the following decades. Despite making the playoffs consistently during this time, they struggled to advance past the first round. In the early 2000s, the team was sold to new ownership, which began a period of rebuilding. The Pistons drafted young talent such as Darko Milicic and Rodney Stuckey, but these picks did not pan out as hoped. The team also made questionable trades, such as the acquisition of Ben Wallace from the Orlando Magic. Despite these setbacks, the Pistons were able to find some success in the late 2000s with the emergence of players like Chauncey Billups and Tayshaun Prince. However, the team continued to struggle in the playoffs, failing to advance past the second round. In recent years, the Pistons have undergone another rebuild, trading away key players such as Andre Drummond and Blake Griffin in an effort to restart their franchise.

6. Recent Years and Future Prospects

The Detroit Pistons have had their fair share of ups and downs over the years, and the past few seasons have been no exception. In recent years, the team has struggled to find consistent success on the court, with some lean seasons and high draft picks that failed to live up to expectations. However, despite these challenges, there is still reason to be optimistic about the future prospects of the Detroit Pistons.

One bright spot in recent years has been the emergence of young talent on the roster. Players like Luke Kennard, Bruce Brown Jr., and Sviatoslav Mykhailiuk have shown flashes of brilliance and have helped keep the team competitive even during tough times. Additionally, the team has made smart moves in the front office, bringing in experienced coaches and executives to guide the franchise back towards success.

Looking ahead to the future, the Detroit Pistons have a number of exciting prospects on the horizon. With another high draft pick this year, the team has the opportunity to add yet another talented player to their already impressive pool of young talent. Additionally, the team has a number of promising free agents set to hit the market, including star players like Blake Griffin and Andre Drummond, who could potentially re-sign with the team or bring in top talent from around the league.

Overall, while the past few years may not have been kind to the Detroit Pistons, there is still plenty of reason to be hopeful about the future. With a strong core of young players and smart management in place, the team is poised to make a comeback and return to its former glory as one of the most successful franchises in NBA history.

7. Key Players and Coaches

The Detroit Pistons have had many notable players and coaches throughout their history. In this section, we will take a closer look at some of the most influential figures in the team's success.

One of the most iconic players in Detroit Pistons history is Isiah Thomas. As a point guard, Thomas was instrumental in leading the team to its first championship in 1989. He was known for his speed, agility, and scoring ability, and was named the NBA Finals MVP that year. Thomas also played a key role in the Pistons' success during the Bad Boys era, using his leadership skills to guide the team through tough times.

Another important player in the team's history is Joe Dumars. As both a player and executive, Dumars played a crucial role in building the Pistons into a championship contender. As a shooting guard, he was a consistent scorer and helped lead the team to the NBA Finals in 1990. After retiring as a player, Dumars became the team's general manager and oversaw several successful draft picks, including Grant Hill and Chauncey Billups.

Other notable players who have donned the Pistons uniform include Dennis Rodman, Vince Ellis, and Bob Lanier. These players, along with others, helped shape the team's identity and made them a force to be reckoned with in the NBA.

In terms of coaching, the Detroit Pistons have had several successful coaches over the years. One of the most notable is Chuck Daly, who led the team to two NBA championships in the 1980s. Daly was known for his defensive strategies and his ability to motivate his players. Other notable coaches include Alvin Gentry, Larry Brown, and Stan Van Gundy.

8. Iconic Moments and Games

The Detroit Pistons have had many iconic moments and games throughout their history. Here are some of the most memorable ones:

1. "The Shot Heard 'Round the World": In 1980, with the score tied at 101, Isiah Thomas hit a buzzer-beating jumper to defeat the Houston Rockets and advance the Pistons to the NBA Finals. This shot has been etched in the memories of Pistons fans ever since.

2. "The Malice at the Palace": On November 19, 2004, during a game against the Indiana Pacers, players from both teams got into a brawl on the court. The altercation resulted in several ejections and suspensions, and it remains one of the most infamous moments in NBA history.

3. "The Double-Double Dynasty": During the 1980s, center Bill Laimbeer and power forward Dennis Rodman led the Pistons to four straight NBA championships, with both players averaging double-doubles in points and rebounds.

4. "The 3-Point Revolution": In the early 2000s, the Pistons became known as the "Golden State Warriors of the East" due to their aggressive full-court press and fast-paced offense, which relied heavily on three-point shooting. They made the playoffs every year from 2000 to 2008, reaching the Eastern Conference Finals in 2008.

5. "The Return of the King": In 2016, after a brief retirement, Tim Duncan returned to the NBA as a coach for the Pistons. Although his tenure was short-lived, he brought a new level of professionalism and discipline to the team.

9. Fan Culture and Traditions

The Detroit Pistons have a passionate fan base known as "Piston Nation." These fans are known for their loyalty and dedication to the team, regardless of their success on the court. One of the most iconic traditions of Piston Nation is the "Victory Cigar," where fans celebrate a win with a cigar. This tradition has been passed down from generation to generation and is a symbol of the team's history and the unwavering support of its fans. Another popular tradition is the "Jalen Rose Garden Party," which takes place at Jalen Rose's home and brings together fans from all over the world to celebrate the team and its players. These traditions are just a few examples of the rich culture and history of the Detroit Pistons and their dedicated fan base.

10. Conclusion

The Detroit Pistons have a rich and colorful history that spans over 75 years. From their early days as a franchise to their current status as one of the most successful teams in NBA history, the Pistons have always been a team to watch. In this article, we have taken a look at some of the key moments and events that have shaped the Pistons' journey, from their early success in the 1980s to their challenges and rebuilding efforts in recent years. We have also explored the team's fan culture and traditions, and highlighted some of the key players and coaches who have helped to make the Pistons the team they are today. As the Pistons continue to move forward, it will be interesting to see what the future holds for this storied franchise.

Detroit's Economic Rebirth Through Basketball: The Story of the Detroit Pistons

1. Introduction

Detroit, once known as the "Motor City," has a rich history in the world of basketball. The Detroit Pistons have been a part of this history since their establishment in 1945. This team has not only brought excitement to the city's residents but has also played a significant role in Detroit's economic rebirth. In this article, we will explore the story of how the Detroit Pistons have contributed to the city's economic growth and revitalization.

2. History of the Detroit Pistons

The Detroit Pistons are one of the most storied franchises in NBA history. Founded in 1945 as the Fort Wayne Zollers, the team relocated to Detroit in 1957 and has been known as the Pistons ever since. Over the years, the team has had its fair share of ups and downs, but it has always remained a beloved part of the Detroit community. In this section, we will explore the history of the Detroit Pistons and how they have become a symbol of hope and resilience for the city of Detroit.

3. Impact of the Detroit Pistons on the city's economy

The Detroit Pistons have had a significant impact on the city's economy, both positive and negative. On one hand, the team has brought in millions of dollars in revenue through ticket sales, merchandise, and other sources. This has helped to boost the local economy and create jobs in the hospitality and retail industries. Additionally, the team has been instrumental in attracting new businesses and investments to the city, as companies look to capitalize on the success of the team and the growing interest in the city. However, there have also been concerns about the financial burden that the team places on the city, particularly in terms of public funding for stadiums and other facilities. Despite these challenges, the Detroit Pistons remain an important part of the city's identity and continue to play a role in its economic development.

4. The rise of the "Bad Boys" era

The "Bad Boys" era refers to the period between 1981 and 1991 when the Detroit Pistons became one of the most dominant teams in NBA history. Led by players like Isiah Thomas, Joe Dumars, and Dennis Rodman, the Pistons won back-to-back championships in 1989 and 1990, and appeared in the Finals again in 1991. During this time, the team had a reputation for being physically tough and aggressive on the court, earning them the nickname "Bad Boys." The success of the team during this era had a significant impact on the city of Detroit, which was struggling economically at the time. The Pistons became a source of pride for the city, and their success helped to lift the spirits of Detroiters during difficult times. Additionally, the team's popularity drew attention from around the world, bringing tourists and revenue to the city.

5. The impact of basketball on Detroit's revitalization

The Detroit Pistons have had a significant impact on the revitalization of Detroit's economy. The team's success on the court has brought attention and investment to the city, helping to spur economic growth and development. The NBA's presence in Detroit has also created jobs and opportunities for residents, both directly through employment with the team and indirectly through the creation of related businesses and services. Additionally, the Pistons have been involved in various community outreach programs, using basketball as a tool for positive change in the city.

6. Current state of the Detroit Pistons and their role in the city's economic growth

The Detroit Pistons have been an integral part of the city's economic growth for decades. Since their founding in 1945, the team has brought in millions of dollars in revenue for the city through ticket sales, merchandise, and other forms of revenue generation. However, in recent years, the team has struggled both on and off the court. Despite this, they continue to play an important role in the city's economic growth.

One way that the Detroit Pistons contribute to the city's economy is through job creation. The team employs hundreds of people in various roles, from players and coaches to support staff and vendors. These jobs not only provide income for local residents, but they also generate additional spending in the community through things like restaurants, hotels, and other businesses catering to the team's needs.

Another way that the Detroit Pistons contribute to the city's economy is through tourism. The team draws fans from all over the region, many of whom come to watch games at Little Caesars Arena or visit other attractions in the area. This influx of visitors generates revenue for local businesses and helps to support the city's hospitality industry.

Finally, the Detroit Pistons also play a role in attracting new businesses and investment to the city. The team's presence in downtown Detroit helps to create a vibrant atmosphere that can be appealing to companies looking to establish a location there. Additionally, the team's ownership group, the Ilitch family, has invested heavily in the city's infrastructure, including the construction of Little Caesars Arena and the renovation of other properties in the area.

Overall, while the current state of the Detroit Pistons may not be as strong as it has been in the past, they still play an important role in the city's economic growth. Through job creation, tourism, and business attraction, the team continues to be a valuable asset to the city.

7. Conclusion

The conclusion of this article highlights the significant role that the Detroit Pistons have played in the city's economic rebirth. From their humble beginnings as a small-time franchise to becoming one of the most successful and influential teams in NBA history, the Pistons have not only brought pride and excitement to the city of Detroit but also helped to drive its economic growth and revitalization. Their success has attracted new businesses, investments, and opportunities to the area, creating jobs and stimulating the local economy. Additionally, the team's commitment to community outreach and youth development programs has had a positive impact on the lives of many young people in Detroit. As the city continues to rebuild and grow, it is clear that the legacy of the Detroit Pistons will continue to be felt for generations to come.

Detroit Pistons' Drafts and Trades: A Look at Their Successes and Challenges

1. Introduction

The Detroit Pistons are a professional basketball team based in Detroit, Michigan. They are members of the National Basketball Association (NBA) and have been since the league's inception in 1945. Throughout their history, the Pistons have had both successful drafts and trades that have helped shape their roster and ultimately their success on the court. In this article, we will take a closer look at some of the most notable successes and challenges in the Pistons' drafts and trades, as well as their overall performance and future outlook.

2. Successes in Drafts

The Detroit Pistons have had several successful draft picks throughout their history. In this section, we will take a closer look at some of their most notable selections and how they have contributed to the team's success.

Andre Drummond:

Drummond was selected ninth overall by the Pistons in the 2012 NBA Draft. He quickly established himself as one of the best young centers in the league, averaging 13.2 points and 12.2 rebounds per game during his rookie season. Drummond has since become a three-time All-Star and a key piece of the Pistons' frontcourt.

Reggie Jackson:

Jackson was drafted by the Oklahoma City Thunder with the 24th pick in the 2011 NBA Draft, but was later traded to the Pistons in 2015.

During his time in Detroit, Jackson averaged 18.8 points and 6.3 assists per game, making him a valuable asset to the team. He was even named the NBA's Most Improved Player in 2017.

Tobias Harris:

Harris was selected with the 19th pick in the 2014 NBA Draft by the Los Angeles Clippers, but was later traded to the Pistons in 2017. Since joining the team, Harris has consistently been one

3. Challenges in Drafts

The Detroit Pistons have had their fair share of challenges when it comes to the NBA draft. Despite making some great picks, they have also made some questionable ones that have hindered their progress. Here are some of the biggest challenges the team has faced in the draft:

1. Kemba Walker trade: In 2018, the Pistons traded away their first-round pick in the NBA draft to the Boston Celtics in exchange for point guard Kyrie Irving. However, this move backfired as Irving requested a trade after just one season with the team, leaving them without a first-round pick.

2. Blake Griffin trade: In 2017, the Pistons traded for All-Star forward Blake Griffin, which looked like a great move at the time. However, injuries limited him to just 25 games in his first season with the team, and he was eventually traded away in 2018.

3. The 2021 NBA Draft: With the COVID-19 pandemic causing uncertainty around the world, the NBA decided to hold a virtual draft instead of the usual in-person event. This made it difficult for teams to scout and evaluate players properly, leading to some questionable picks being made.

4. Other notable draft picks: While the Pistons have made some good draft picks, such as Andre Drummond, Reggie Jackson, Tobias Harris, and Jerami Grant, they have also missed out on some top talents due to poor luck or bad decision-making. For example, they passed on drafting Steph Curry in 2009, and they also missed out on drafting Kevin Durant in 2007.

4. Successes in Trades

The Detroit Pistons have had several successful trades throughout their history. Some notable examples include:

* Acquiring Josh Smith: In 2013, the Pistons traded for Josh Smith, who was coming off a career year with the Atlanta Hawks. Smith proved to be a valuable addition to the team, averaging 12.7 points and 7.4 rebounds per game during his two seasons in Detroit.

* Dealing for Jimmy Butler: In 2017, the Pistons made a bold move by trading for Jimmy Butler, who was coming off a playoff appearance with the Chicago Bulls. Butler helped lead the Pistons to the playoffs that season and continued to be a key player for the team until he was traded to the Brooklyn Nets in 2019.

* The acquisition of Derrick Rose: In 2016, the Pistons signed Derrick Rose to a contract extension. While Rose struggled with injuries during his time in Detroit, he still managed to average 18.1 points and 4.4 assists per game in his first season with the team.

5. Challenges in Trades

The Detroit Pistons have faced several challenges in their trades over the years. One major challenge was the trade of Greg Monroe, which many felt was a mistake. Another challenge was the Stan Van Gundy era trades, which were criticized for being too focused on salary cap management rather than player development. Additionally, the team's performance at the 2020 NBA Trade Deadline was lackluster, with few notable acquisitions made. Despite these challenges, the Pistons have also had some successful trades, such as acquiring Josh Smith and dealing for Jimmy Butler. Overall, the team's approach to trades has been mixed, with both successes and failures.

6. Overall Performance

The Detroit Pistons have had a mixed record of success in recent years. While they have made some notable acquisitions through drafts and trades, there have been some missteps as well. In this section, we will take a closer look at the team's overall performance and assess how it compares to other teams in the league.

One area where the Pistons have struggled is in player development. Many talented players have come through the organization, but few have reached their full potential. This has led to a revolving door of players coming and going, with little consistency in the roster. Additionally, the team has struggled to find a consistent coach who can lead them to success.

Despite these challenges, the Pistons have managed to make the playoffs in some seasons. However, they have not been able to advance past the first round, which has been a major disappointment for fans. Compared to other teams in the league, the Pistons' overall performance has been mediocre at best. They have not been able to consistently challenge for championships, and their lack of success has led to a loss of fan interest and support.

Looking ahead, the future outlook for the Pistons is uncertain. While there are some promising young players on the roster, the team will need to make some significant changes if they hope to improve their performance. This may include making some tough decisions regarding player contracts and coaching staff. Ultimately, the success of the team will depend on their ability to find a balance between talent and cohesion, and to develop a strong, stable leadership structure.

7. Future Outlook

The future outlook not so good.

8. Conclusion

In conclusion, the Detroit Pistons have had both successes and challenges in their drafts and trades over the years. From Andre Drummond and Reggie Jackson to Kemba Walker and Blake Griffin, the team has made some notable acquisitions through the draft and trade process. However, they have also faced setbacks with trades such as the Greg Monroe deal and the Stan Van Gundy era trades.

The team's overall performance in recent years has been mixed, with some successful seasons followed by periods of struggle. Moving forward, it will be interesting to see how the team approaches future drafts and trades, and what strategies they implement to continue their success or work towards rebuilding. Ultimately, the Detroit Pistons' drafts and trades serve as a case study for the importance of careful decision-making and risk management in professional sports.

The Detroit Pistons' Cultural Legacy: Celebrating Diversity Through Basketball

1. Introduction

The Detroit Pistons have always been more than just a basketball team. Since their inception in 1945, they have served as a symbol of hope, perseverance, and diversity in a city known for its struggles. This article celebrates the cultural legacy of the Detroit Pistons, highlighting their impact on the sport of basketball, popular culture, and the community at large. From their early years to their championship wins, this article explores the many facets of the Detroit Pistons' legacy and what it means to the city of Detroit and beyond.

2. Early Years of the Detroit Pistons

The Detroit Pistons were founded in 1945 as part of the National Basketball League (NBL). They later joined the NBA when it was formed in 1949. Over the years, the team has had its fair share of ups and downs, but their impact on basketball culture cannot be denied.

In the early days of the Detroit Pistons, the team was predominantly white. However, they made history when they signed their first African American player, Chuck Cooper, in 1957. This move paved the way for greater diversity in the league and helped break down barriers in sports.

Cooper played for the Pistons from 1957 to 1960, and although he was not a star player, his signing was a significant moment in NBA history. It marked the beginning of a shift towards greater inclusion and representation in the sport.

Over time, the Detroit Pistons continued to build a diverse roster, with players from all over the world joining the team. This helped to create a unique identity for the franchise and contributed to their success on the court.

3. Expansion and Diversity in Roster

The Detroit Pistons have always been at the forefront of diversity in basketball, and this has been especially evident in their roster. Over the years, the team has expanded its reach and brought in players from all corners of the world, creating a truly global presence on the court. One of the most notable moments in this expansion came when the team signed the first openly gay player in NBA history, making a bold statement about inclusivity and acceptance. This move not only showed the world that the Detroit Pistons were committed to diversity, but it also paved the way for other teams to follow suit. Today, the Pistons continue to be a leader in promoting diversity and inclusion both on and off the court.

4. Community Engagement and Social Justice

The Detroit Pistons have always been committed to giving back to their community. They have partnered with various organizations to support social justice initiatives and promote diversity and inclusion. For example, they have worked with the Rosa Parks Foundation to promote civil rights and equality. Additionally, they have supported LGBTQ+ rights through partnerships with organizations such as the Human Rights Campaign. Their dedication to these causes has helped to further the team's cultural legacy in basketball.

5. Impact on Popular Culture

The Detroit Pistons have had a significant impact on popular culture beyond the world of basketball. Their fashion choices, both on and off the court, have influenced trends across the globe. From the "Air Jordan" sneakers worn by Michael Jordan during his time with the team to the bold and bright colors of their uniforms, the Pistons have always been at the forefront of style.

In addition to their influence on fashion, the Pistons have also made appearances in various forms of media, including movies and television shows. Their championship runs and larger-than-life personalities have made them a favorite among fans and non-fans alike.

Overall, the Detroit Pistons have left an indelible mark on popular culture, inspiring countless individuals to embrace their unique style and personality.

6. Team Success and Legacy

The Detroit Pistons have had a storied history in the NBA, with a number of successful seasons and championship wins under their belt. This section will explore the team's legacy and how it has impacted the league as a whole. From the early days of the team to the present day, we will look at the players who have donned the Pistons jersey and made a name for themselves in the world of basketball. We will also discuss the team's impact on popular culture and how they have influenced fashion and media. Finally, we will examine the future of the Detroit Pistons and what fans can expect from this iconic franchise moving forward.

7. Future of the Detroit Pistons

The future of the Detroit Pistons looks bright as they continue to build through their rebuilding efforts. With talented young players and strategic acquisitions, the team has the potential to return to championship form. Fans remain hopeful and excited for what the future holds for this beloved franchise.

8. Conclusion

The Detroit Pistons have left an indelible mark on the world of basketball, not just through their impressive record of victories, but also through their commitment to celebrating diversity and inclusion. From the early days of the team, when they broke barriers by signing the first African American player, to their more recent partnerships with local organizations and support for LGBTQ+ rights, the Detroit Pistons have consistently demonstrated their dedication to making a positive impact in their community. As the team continues to rebuild and strive for success, they remain a shining example of the power of sports to bring people together and inspire change.

9. Poem

A Dream of Glory

In the city of Detroit, where the streets are tough

And the people are strong, there's a team that's rough

The Detroit Pistons, they play with heart

Bringing pride to their community, never to depart

From the early days, when they first took the floor

To the championship wins that brought them more

They've celebrated diversity, breaking barriers galore

A true symbol of unity, forevermore

With players from all corners of the globe

They've shown the world what it means to be a pro

From the court to the community, they give their all

A dream of glory, for everyone to see and share

So here's to the Detroit Pistons, a team of great worth

Their legacy lives on, forever enshrined in sport

Celebrating diversity, through basketball they unite

A shining star, forever in our hearts, tonight

10. Short Story

The Detroit Pistons were once known as one of the most diverse teams in the NBA. They had players from all corners of the world, each bringing their unique skills and cultures to the court. In this short story, we follow the journey of one such player, a young man named Ahmed who left his home in Egypt to pursue his dream of playing professional basketball in America.

Ahmed had always been fascinated by the game of basketball, watching it on TV and playing with friends whenever he could. He was small for his age, but he had a quick jump shot and a natural feel for the game. When he heard about tryouts for a new basketball team in Detroit, he knew he had to go.

He arrived at the gym, nervous but determined. There were dozens of other players there, all hoping to make the cut. But when it came time for Ahmed to show off his skills, he blew everyone away. His shots were precise and powerful, and he moved around the court with grace and agility.

After the tryout, the coach called Ahmed aside. "You have real talent," he said. "But I don't think you're ready for the NBA yet."

Ahmed was disappointed, but he didn't give up. He worked harder than ever, honing his skills and learning from the older players on the team. And eventually, his hard work paid off. The Detroit Pistons signed him to a contract, and he became one of the top players on the team.

As he took the court for his first game, Ahmed felt a sense of pride and accomplishment that he had never felt before. He looked out at the crowd and saw people of all ages and backgrounds cheering him on. It was then that he realized the true power of basketball - not just as a sport, but as a tool for bringing people together.

And so, every time he stepped onto the court, Ahmed played with everything he had, knowing that he represented not just himself, but his entire community. He may have been small, but he was a giant in the world of basketball, and he would do everything in his power to make sure that the Detroit Pistons remained a symbol of diversity and inclusion for years to come.

Detroit Pistons: The Palace Era

1. Introduction to the Detroit Pistons

The Detroit Pistons are a professional basketball team based in Detroit, Michigan. They began play in the National Basketball Association (NBA) in 1945 as the Fort Wayne Pistons before moving to Detroit in 1957. The Pistons have had a rich history in the NBA, with several successful seasons and iconic moments. In this article, we will explore one of the most memorable eras in Pistons history: the Palace Era.

2. History of the Palace of Auburn Hills

The Palace of Auburn Hills was a state-of-the-art arena located in Auburn Hills, Michigan, that served as the home court for the Detroit Pistons from 1978 to 2017. It was named after the nearby Palace of Windsor, which was once the residence of Henry VIII. The arena had a seating capacity of over 20,000 and was known for its luxurious amenities and excellent acoustics. The Palace of Auburn Hills played host to many memorable moments in Pistons history, including the team's back-to-back championships in 1989 and 1990.

3. The rise of the "Bad Boys" era

The "Bad Boys" era of the Detroit Pistons began in the late 1980s and lasted through the early 1990s. During this time, the team became known for their physical play and aggressive defense, which intimidated opponents and helped them win three NBA championships. Key players during this era included Isiah Thomas, Joe Dumars, and Rick Mahorn. The team's toughness and intensity were personified by coach Chuck Daly, who implemented a hard-nosed style of play that emphasized defense and rebounding. The "Bad Boys" reputation was solidified when the team won back-to-back championships in 1989 and 1990, and again in 1998. Despite controversy surrounding some of their tactics, the "Bad Boys" remain one of the most iconic teams in NBA history.

4. Key players during the Palace Era

During the Palace Era, several key players helped shape the team into one of the most dominant forces in the NBA. Here are some of the standout performers during this time period:

1. Isiah Thomas - Known as the face of the Bad Boys, Thomas was a fierce competitor who led the team in scoring during the 1988-1989 season with an average of 22.2 points per game. He also averaged 6.3 assists and 1.9 steals during that same season.

2. Joe Dumars - Another key member of the Bad Boys, Dumars was known for his clutch shooting and lockdown defense. He won three championships with the Pistons and was named the NBA Finals MVP in 1989.

3. Dennis Rodman - Although he only played five seasons with the Pistons, Rodman made a lasting impact on the team during the Palace Era. His rebounding prowess and defensive skills were crucial to the team's success.

4. Bill Laimbeer - Known for his physical play and toughness, Laimbeer was a dominant force in the paint during the Bad Boys era. He was a two-time All-Star and helped anchor the team's defense.

5. Vinnie Johnson - Known as "The Microwave," Johnson provided instant offense off the bench during the Palace Era. He was a four-time NBA champion and scored over 10,000 points in his career.

5. Coaching changes during the Palace Era

The Detroit Pistons experienced several coaching changes during the Palace Era. One of the most notable was the departure of head coach Chuck Daly in 1992, who was replaced by his assistant coach, Don Chaney. Chaney led the team to the Eastern Conference Finals in his first season as head coach, but the team struggled in subsequent years. In 1995, Chaney was fired and replaced by Alvin Gentry, who had previously served as an assistant coach under Daly. Gentry guided the team to the playoffs in each of his first three seasons, but he was fired after the 1998 season. In 1999, Rick Carlisle was hired as head coach, and he led the team to the NBA Finals in his first season. However, the team lost to the Los Angeles Lakers in four games. After a disappointing start to the 2000 season, Carlisle was fired and replaced by Larry Brown, who had previously coached the Pistons during the early 1990s. Brown led the team to the Eastern Conference Finals in his first season, but the team failed to make the playoffs in subsequent years. In 2003, Brown resigned and was replaced by Flip Saunders, who had previously played for the Pistons during the late 1980s. Saunders led the team to the playoffs in each of his first two seasons, but he was fired after the 2005 season. In 2006, Michael Curry was hired as head coach, and he led the team to the Eastern Conference Finals in his first season. However, the team struggled in subsequent years, and Curry was fired after the 2008 season. In 2009, John Kuester was hired as head coach, and he led the team to the playoffs in his first season. However, the team struggled in the playoffs, and Kuester was fired after the 2010 season. In 2011, Lawrence Frank was hired as head coach, and he led the team to the playoffs in each of his first three seasons. However, the team struggled in the playoffs, and Frank was fired after the 2013 season. In 2014, Stan Van Gundy was hired as head coach, and he led the team to the playoffs in each of his first two seasons. However, the team struggled in the playoffs, and Van Gundy was fired after the 2018 season. In 2019, Dwane Casey was hired as head coach, and he led the team to the playoffs in each of his first two seasons.

6. The impact of the Palace Era on the NBA

The Palace Era had a significant impact on the NBA, shaping the league in numerous ways. One of the most notable effects was the increased popularity of the sport, both in Detroit and across the country. The rivalries between the Pistons and their opponents, particularly the Celtics, were intense and highly publicized, drawing large crowds and generating excitement for the game. Additionally, the physical play and aggressive style of the Pistons during this era helped to redefine the way basketball was played, paving the way for the modern NBA. Furthermore, the success of the Pistons during the Palace Era inspired other teams to adopt a similar tough, hard-nosed approach, leading to a shift in the league's culture. Overall, the impact of the Palace Era on the NBA was immense, leaving a lasting legacy on the sport.

7. Memorable moments from the Palace Era

The Detroit Pistons' time at the Palace of Auburn Hills was filled with many memorable moments. From the team's championship runs to individual performances, there were plenty of highlights to choose from. Here are some of the most memorable moments from the Palace Era:

* In Game 6 of the 1989 Eastern Conference Finals against the Chicago Bulls, Isiah Thomas scored 25 points in the fourth quarter to lead the Pistons to a 107-105 victory and force a Game 7. This performance cemented Thomas' legacy as one of the greatest point guards in NBA history.

* During the 1990 season, the Pistons went on a 35-game winning streak, which still stands as an NBA record. This run included several dominant victories over top teams like the Los Angeles Lakers and Boston Celtics.

* In the 1991 playoffs, the Pistons defeated the Los Angeles Lakers in five games to win their first championship since 1989. This series featured several classic matchups between the Pistons and Lakers, including a Game 5 that went into triple overtime.

* During the 1992 playoffs, the Pistons once again made it to the finals, where they faced the Chicago Bulls. Despite losing the series in six games, the Pistons put up a strong fight and showed that they were a force to be reckoned with in the league.

* One of the most iconic moments from the Palace Era came in Game 5 of the 1991 Eastern Conference Finals against the New York Knicks. With the score tied at 104-all, Pistons center Bill Laimbeer stole the ball from Knicks guard Pat Riley and dunked it to give Detroit a 106-104 lead. The Pistons would go on to win the game and eventually the championship.

8. Challenges faced during the Palace Era

The Detroit Pistons experienced several challenges during their time at the Palace of Auburn Hills. One of the biggest challenges was maintaining success on the court. Despite having talented players like Isiah Thomas, Joe Dumars, and Dennis Rodman, the team struggled to consistently perform well in the playoffs. In fact, they didn't win an NBA championship until 1989, when they defeated the Los Angeles Lakers in four games. Additionally, the team had to deal with off-court issues such as player contract disputes and controversies surrounding coach Chuck Daly. Another challenge was the high cost of tickets and luxury suites, which made it difficult for some fans to attend games. However, despite these challenges, the Palace Era remains one of the most iconic periods in Detroit Pistons history.

9. Reflections on the Palace Era

The Palace Era was a time of great success for the Detroit Pistons, as they won two NBA championships in 1989 and 1990. However, it was also a time of controversy and criticism. Many fans and analysts have reflected on the impact of the Palace Era on the league and its players. Some have praised the toughness and grit of the "Bad Boys," while others have criticized their tactics and behavior. Regardless of one's opinion, the Palace Era will always be remembered as a pivotal moment in NBA history.

10. Conclusion

The conclusion of the Detroit Pistons' time at the Palace of Auburn Hills marks the end of an era in NBA history. The team's success during this time period was unprecedented, and the impact it had on the league cannot be overstated. From the "Bad Boys" era to the coaching changes and memorable moments, the Palace Era will always be remembered as one of the most exciting and successful periods in Detroit Pistons' history. While there were challenges faced during this time, the team persevered and continued to dominate on the court. As the team moves forward to their new home, they will carry with them the memories and lessons learned from the Palace Era, and continue to strive for greatness.

The Heated History of Detroit Pistons Rivalries

1. Introduction to the Detroit Pistons and their history in basketball

The Detroit Pistons are a professional basketball team based in Detroit, Michigan. They are members of the National Basketball Association (NBA) and have been since the league's founding in 1946. Throughout their history, the Pistons have had many memorable moments and iconic players, including Isiah Thomas, Joe Dumars, and Chauncey Billups. However, one aspect of the Pistons' history that stands out above all others is their long and storied rivalries with other teams in the NBA. In this article, we will explore the heated history of Detroit Pistons rivalries, from their early days in the league to the present day.

2. Overview of rivalries within the NBA

The National Basketball Association (NBA) has a rich history of intense rivalries between its teams. These rivalries often stem from geographic proximity, shared successes or failures, and contrasting playing styles. Some of the most notable rivalries in NBA history have been between the Boston Celtics and the Los Angeles Lakers, but there are many others that have left a lasting impact on the league. In this section, we will provide an overview of some of the most significant rivalries within the NBA.

3. The rise of the "Bad Boys" era and the emergence of the Detroit Pistons as a dominant force

During the late 1980s and early 1990s, the Detroit Pistons became one of the most feared teams in the NBA due to their aggressive and physical playing style, earning them the nickname "The Bad Boys." Led by stars like Isiah Thomas, Joe Dumars, and Dennis Rodman, the Pistons dominated the league, winning back-to-back championships in 1989 and 1990, and reaching the Finals again in 1991. Their tough defense and fearless attitude intimidated opponents and solidified the team's reputation as a force to be reckoned with. The Bad Boys era was a turning point in Detroit Pistons history, establishing them as a powerhouse and setting the stage for future rivalries.

4. The rivalry with the Boston Celtics during the Bad Boys era

The rivalry between the Detroit Pistons and the Boston Celtics during the Bad Boys era was one of the most intense and memorable in NBA history. The two teams faced off numerous times during the 1980s and early 1990s, with each game being highly anticipated and often filled with physical play and animosity.

The Detroit Pistons, led by players such as Isiah Thomas, Joe Dumars, and Dennis Rodman, became known as the "Bad Boys" due to their aggressive and physical playing style. They were not afraid to use their size and strength to intimidate opponents, and they were known for their hard-nosed defense and relentless pressure on the ball.

The Boston Celtics, on the other hand, were led by legendary coach Red Auerbach and a talented roster that included Larry Bird, Kevin McHale, and Robert Parish. While the Celtics were known for their skill and precision on offense, they were also not afraid to get physical when necessary.

When these two teams met on the court, it was always a battle. The games were marked by fierce competition, physical play, and plenty of trash talking. There were many memorable moments in this rivalry, including several instances of flagrant fouls, technical fouls, and even ejections.

One of the most infamous moments in the rivalry came during a game between the two teams in 1984. With less than a minute remaining in the game, Isiah Thomas was fouled by Danny Ainge and hit his head on the floor. Thomas suffered a concussion and had to be taken out of the game, leading to accusations that the Celtics had intentionally tried to hurt him. This incident only added fuel to the already intense rivalry between the two teams.

Despite the intensity of the rivalry, there were also moments of respect between the players. Both sides acknowledged the talent and skill of the other, and there were several instances of players from both teams shaking hands or exchanging words of admiration after a particularly hard-fought game.

Overall, the rivalry between the Detroit Pistons and the Boston Celtics during the Bad Boys era was one of the most intense and memorable in NBA history. It epitomized the physical and competitive nature of the sport, and it remains a favorite memory for many fans of both teams.

5. The rivalry with the Chicago Bulls during the Bad Boys era

The rivalry between the Detroit Pistons and the Chicago Bulls during the Bad Boys era was one of the most intense and fiercely competitive in

NBA history. The two teams faced off numerous times during the late 1980s and early 1990s, with each game feeling like a playoff matchup.

The animosity between the two teams began in the 1984 draft, when the Pistons selected future Hall of Fame center Bill Laimbeer with the third overall pick, while the Bulls chose forward Charles Oakley at number seven. This move set the stage for years of bitter rivalry, with both teams vying for supremacy in the Eastern Conference.

In the 1987-88 season, the Pistons and Bulls met in the playoffs for the first time since the draft. The series was marked by physical play, hard fouls, and plenty of trash talking. The Pistons emerged victorious, winning the series in five games.

The following year, the two teams met again in the playoffs, this time with the Bulls looking to avenge their loss. The series was just as intense as the previous one, with both teams battling for every possession. In Game 5, the Pistons famously used a "Jordan Rules" strategy to limit Michael Jordan's effectiveness, leading to a 95-91 victory and a series win for Detroit.

The rivalry between the Pistons and Bulls continued throughout the Bad Boys era, with each team trying to one-up the other on the court. The animosity between the two teams was so great that it spilled over into the locker room, with players from both sides engaging in heated exchanges.

Despite the intense rivalry, however, the Pistons and Bulls ultimately had a lot of respect for each other. Both teams were known for their toughness and physical play, and they helped to elevate the level of competition in the NBA during the Bad Boys era.

Today, the rivalry between the Pistons and Bulls remains one of the most iconic in NBA history. While the players may have changed, the passion and intensity of those early meetings continue to inspire new generations of fans.

6. The rivalry with the Los Angeles Lakers during the Bad Boys era

The rivalry between the Detroit Pistons and the Los Angeles Lakers during the Bad Boys era was one of the most intense and memorable in NBA history. The two teams faced off numerous times in the playoffs, with each game being filled with physical battles, hard-nosed defense, and high-stakes drama.

The Bad Boys Pistons were known for their tough, physical style of play, which often resulted in rough fouls and technical fouls. This led to several heated confrontations with the Lakers, who were also notorious for their aggressive playing style. One of the most infamous moments in this rivalry occurred in Game 5 of the 1988 NBA Finals, when Lakers center Mychal Thompson and Pistons forward Dennis Rodman got into a physical altercation after a foul was called against Rodman.

Despite the animosity between the two teams, there were also moments of respect and admiration. Both the Pistons and the Lakers were among the best teams in the league during the Bad Boys era, and they both had a deep appreciation for the game of basketball. This respect was evident in their many battles on the court, which helped to elevate the NBA to new heights of popularity and excitement.

Overall, the rivalry between the Detroit Pistons and the Los Angeles Lakers during the Bad Boys era was a defining moment in the history of the NBA. It showcased the physical and emotional intensity that can be found in professional sports, while also highlighting the respect and admiration that even the fiercest rivals can have for each other.

7. The impact of the Bad Boys era on the sport of basketball

The Bad Boys era had a profound impact on the sport of basketball, both positive and negative. On one hand, the physical style of play employed by the Pistons during this time period helped to usher in a new era of toughness and intensity in the league. Players were encouraged to play aggressively and to protect their teammates at all costs, leading to a more physical and competitive brand of basketball. This style of play was emulated by other teams around the league, and the Bad Boys era became synonymous with hard-nosed, gritty basketball.

On the other hand, the rough and tumble nature of the Bad Boys era led to some controversial incidents on the court. There were numerous instances of flagrant fouls, technical fouls, and even players being ejected from games. This led to concerns about the safety of the players and the need for stricter enforcement of the rules. Additionally, some fans and media members criticized the Pistons for being too physical and not playing the game the right way.

Despite these controversies, the Bad Boys era remains a significant chapter in the history of the Detroit Pistons and the NBA. It helped to shape the league into what it is today, and its legacy can still be felt in the way that players approach the game.

8. The evolution of Detroit Pistons rivalries beyond the Bad Boys era

After the heyday of the "Bad Boys" era, the Detroit Pistons continued to be a formidable team in the NBA, but their rivalries shifted focus. One notable rivalry that emerged during this time was with the Indiana Pacers. This rivalry was fueled by the physical play and intensity of both teams, and it often resulted in highly competitive games. Another rivalry that developed was with the Toronto Raptors, which gained steam in the early 2000s when the Raptors began to challenge the Pistons for supremacy in the Eastern Conference. The Raptors' success, coupled with the Pistons' decline, led to a fierce rivalry between the two teams.

9. Current rivalries and the legacy of the Detroit Pistons' heated history

The Detroit Pistons have a rich history of rivalries, both past and present. While the team's most iconic rivalries date back to the Bad Boys era, there are still several current rivalries that carry on the legacy of heated competition.

One of the most notable current rivalries is between the Pistons and the Cleveland Cavaliers. This rivalry began in 2003 when LeBron James, who would later become a four-time MVP and four-time NBA champion, was drafted first overall by the Cleveland Cavaliers. Since then, the two teams have faced off numerous times in playoff series, including a memorable seven-game series in 2007.

Another current rivalry for the Pistons is with the Milwaukee Bucks. This rivalry has been brewing since the early 2000s, when the Bucks were led by former Piston Tayshaun Prince. In recent years, the two teams have met in the playoffs multiple times, with each game being highly competitive and intense.

Despite the emergence of these new rivalries, the legacy of the Bad Boys era remains a significant factor in the Pistons' identity. Fans and players alike continue to reference the toughness, intensity, and physicality of the Bad Boys era, which helped to shape the culture of the NBA.

In conclusion, while the Detroit Pistons may not have the same level of rivalries as they did during the Bad Boys era, the legacy of those rivalries continues to influence the team's identity and approach to the game.

The current rivalries with the Cleveland Cavaliers and Milwaukee Bucks serve as reminders of the Pistons' storied history and their place as one of the most respected franchises in the league.

10. Conclusion on the enduring significance of Detroit Pistons rivalries in the world of basketball

Detroit Pistons rivalries have been a staple of the NBA since the team's inception. From the early days of the league to the present, the Pistons have faced off against some of the most storied franchises in basketball history. While the rivalries of the past may have faded into memory, the impact they had on the sport cannot be overstated. The Bad Boys era, in particular, cemented the Pistons' place as a dominant force and set the stage for future generations of players and fans. Today, the Pistons continue to face off against fierce rivals both old and new, and their legacy as a team that plays hard and never gives up lives on. In conclusion, the enduring significance of Detroit Pistons rivalries lies not just in the excitement they provide on the court, but in the way they have shaped the sport of basketball and inspired generations of players and fans.

Detroit Pistons Icons: Celebrating the Greatest Moments in Team History

1. The 1989 NBA Finals

The 1989 NBA Finals were a historic moment in Detroit Pistons history. Led by legendary coach Chuck Daly and superstar center Isaiah Thomas, the Pistons defeated the Los Angeles Lakers in four games to win their first NBA championship since 1980. The series was marked by incredible defense, clutch performances, and unforgettable moments. One of the most memorable moments came in Game 3, when Thomas hit a buzzer-beating jumper to secure a crucial victory for Detroit. The Pistons went on to win the next two games as well, securing their spot in NBA lore.

2. The "Going Streaking" Era

The "Going Streaking" Era refers to the period of time between 1988 and 1991 when the Detroit Pistons dominated the NBA with their exceptional play on the court. During this era, the team won three consecutive NBA championships and established themselves as one of the greatest teams in NBA history. Led by legendary coach Chuck Daly and superstar center Isaiah Thomas, the Pistons were known for their tough, physical style of play and their ability to execute on both ends of the court. They defeated some of the best teams in the league during this time, including the Los Angeles Lakers and the Boston Celtics, and cemented their place in basketball history with their impressive run of success.

3. The "Fab Five" Era

The "Fab Five" era refers to the period between 1991 and 1994 when the Detroit Pistons had one of the most iconic and successful teams in NBA history. Led by head coach Chuck Daly and featuring five freshman stars, the team revolutionized basketball with their unique style of play, known as "Fast Break." This era saw the Pistons win back-to-back championships in 1990 and 1991, cementing their place in NBA history.

4. The Bad Boy Era

The Bad Boy Era of the Detroit Pistons was one of the most iconic periods in team history. Led by legendary coach Chuck Daly and featuring some of the toughest players in NBA history, the Pistons became known as the "Bad Boys" due to their physical play and aggressive defense. This era saw the Pistons win back-to-back championships in 1989 and 1990, and they continued to dominate the league throughout the 1990s. Some of the key players during this time included Isiah Thomas, Joe Dumars, and Dennis Rodman, who all made significant contributions to the team's success. The Bad Boy Era was not only a time of great triumphs on the court, but it also helped to shape the culture of the NBA and set the stage for future generations of players and fans.

5. The 2004 NBA Championship Run

The 2004 NBA Championship Run was one of the most memorable moments in Detroit Pistons history. Led by superstar point guard Chauncey Billups, the Pistons went on a remarkable run through the playoffs, defeating the Indiana Pacers in seven games in the first round, the New Jersey Nets in five games in the second round, and the Boston Celtics in six games in the Eastern Conference Finals. In the NBA Finals, the Pistons faced off against the Los Angeles Lakers, who were led by Kobe Bryant and Shaquille O'Neal. Despite being heavily favored, the

Lakers were unable to overcome the Pistons' tenacious defense and clutch shooting, as Detroit won the championship in four games. Billups was named the Finals MVP, cementing his status as one of the greatest players in team history.

6. The 2007 NBA Finals

The 2007 NBA Finals was a historic moment for the Detroit Pistons. After a long season of hard-fought battles, the team made it to the championship series against the Golden State Warriors. Led by superstars Chauncey Billups and Richard Hamilton, the Pistons were determined to bring a championship back to Detroit. In a thrilling seven-game series, the Pistons emerged victorious, winning their first championship since 1990. The team's gritty defense and clutch shooting carried them through to a memorable victory, cementing their place in Pistons history as one of the greatest teams ever.

7. The 2019 NBA Playoffs

Detroit Pistons fans were on the edge of their seats as the team made a surprise run through the playoffs in 2019. Led by star players Blake Griffin and Andre Drummond, the Pistons upset several higher-seeded teams en route to the Eastern Conference Finals. Despite falling short against the Milwaukee Bucks, the team's performance during the playoffs was nothing short of remarkable. It was a testament to the hard work and dedication of the players, as well as the coaching staff. Fans were left feeling proud and hopeful for the future of the franchise.

8. The 2021 NBA Bubble Experience

The 2021 NBA Bubble Experience was a unique and unforgettable moment in Detroit Pistons history. For the first time ever, the NBA held its entire playoff tournament at a single location, known as the "bubble."

This was done to minimize the risk of COVID-19 transmission between teams and their families.

The experience was unlike any other, with players and staff living and working in a secure environment for several weeks. Games were played in front of empty arenas, with fans watching on TV and online. Despite the unusual circumstances, the Pistons put on some memorable performances, including a thrilling upset victory over the top-seeded Milwaukee Bucks in the first round.

One of the most memorable moments of the bubble came when Blake Griffin hit a game-winning shot against the Brooklyn Nets in the second round. The shot sent the Pistons through to the Eastern Conference Finals, where they ultimately fell to the eventual champions, the Miami Heat.

Overall, the 2021 NBA Bubble Experience was a challenging but rewarding time for the Detroit Pistons. It showed the resilience and determination of the team and its players, and it will be remembered as one of the most unique and exciting chapters in team history.

9. Other Notable Moments

In addition to the moments mentioned above, there have been many other notable moments in Detroit Pistons history. From the team's first championship in 1989 to their most recent playoff appearance in 2021, the Pistons have provided fans with countless memorable moments. Some of these moments include:

* The 1990 NBA All-Star Game, which was held at the Joe Louis Arena and featured a legendary performance from Isiah Thomas

* The 1998 NBA Draft, where the Pistons selected Darko Milicic with the second overall pick

* The 2008 NBA Draft, where the Pistons selected Greg Monroe with the seventh overall pick

* The 2016 NBA Draft, where the Pistons selected Stanley Johnson with the eighth overall pick

* The 2018 NBA Draft, where the Pistons selected Bruce Brown Jr. with the 28th overall pick

* The 2019 NBA Draft, where the Pistons selected Sekou Doumbouya with the 15th overall pick

* The 2020 NBA Draft, where the Pistons selected Killian Hayes with the seventh overall pick

* The 2021 NBA Draft, where the Pistons selected Jalen Duren with the 13th overall pick

These moments, while not as significant as some of the others on this list, still hold a special place in the hearts of Pistons fans. Whether it's the excitement of draft night or the thrill of seeing a young player make his NBA debut, these moments remind us why we love the game of basketball and the Detroit Pistons in particular.

10. Conclusion

The Detroit Pistons have a rich history filled with memorable moments and iconic players. From the 1989 NBA Finals to the 2021 NBA Bubble Experience, the team has seen its fair share of triumphs and challenges. In this article, we have celebrated some of the greatest moments in Detroit Pistons history, including the "Going Streaking" era, the "Fab Five" era, the Bad Boy Era, the 2004 NBA Championship Run, the 2007 NBA Finals, the 2019 NBA Playoffs, and the 2021 NBA Bubble Experience. We have also touched on other notable moments in team history. It's clear that the Detroit Pistons have left their mark on the NBA, and their legacy continues to inspire fans today.

Rise of the Pistons: The 2000s Era

1. Introduction to the 2000s era

The 2000s era was a time of great change and growth. It was a decade marked by the rise of new technologies, the changing landscape of music and entertainment, and the emergence of new fashion trends. In this article, we will explore the many facets of the 2000s era, from its political and economic changes to its social issues and the impact of the internet on society. We will also examine the advancements made in science and medicine during this time period. Whether you're looking to relive your youth or simply curious about what life was like a decade ago, this article will provide a comprehensive overview of the 2000s era.

2. The rise of technology in the 2000s

The 2000s were a decade of rapid technological advancement. From the dawn of the new millennium to the end of the decade, the world was transformed by the rise of the digital age. In this section, we will explore some of the key technological developments that defined the 2000s.

3. Music and entertainment in the 2000s

The 2000s were a time of great change in the music industry. With the rise of digital technology, artists were able to produce and distribute their music more easily than ever before. This led to a proliferation of new genres and subgenres, as well as a greater diversity of voices in the industry.

One of the most significant developments in music during this time was the emergence of online music stores and streaming services. These platforms allowed fans to access a vast library of music from around the world, and made it easier for independent artists to get their music heard.

In terms of popular music, the 2000s saw the rise of artists like Justin Timberlake, Beyonce, and Usher, who dominated the charts with their infectious pop hits. Meanwhile, hip hop continued to be a dominant force in the industry, with artists like Jay-Z, Kanye West, and Eminem releasing groundbreaking albums that cemented their places as some of the greatest rappers of all time.

In addition to music, the 2000s were also a time of great innovation in the world of entertainment. The rise of reality TV shows and social media platforms gave rise to a new generation of celebrities, many of whom became household names overnight. These influencers and personalities helped to shape the cultural landscape of the decade, and continue to have a lasting impact on the way we consume media today.

4. Fashion trends in the 2000s

The 2000s were a decade of bold fashion choices and experimental styles. From low-rise jeans to Ugg boots, the 2000s saw it all. Here are some of the most memorable fashion trends from the 2000s decade:

1. High-waisted pants: In the early 2000s, high-waisted pants were all the rage. These pants were often paired with crop tops or tube tops, creating a unique and attention-grabbing look.

2. Cropped tops: Another popular style from the 2000s was cropped tops. These tops were often worn over tank tops or sports bras, and were paired with everything from mini skirts to denim shorts.

3. Platform shoes: Platform shoes made a comeback in the 2000s, with many people opting for chunky sneakers or Mary Janes with thick soles.

4. Hoodies: Hoodies were a staple in the 2000s, and were often worn as a casual, everyday garment. They were worn by both men and women and came in a variety of colors and designs.

5. Denim jackets: Denim jackets were another popular item in the 2000s. They were often worn over t-shirts or blouses, and came in a range of colors and washes.

6. Mini skirts: Mini skirts were a staple in the 2000s, and were often worn with cropped tops or tights. They were a popular choice among both younger and older generations.

7. Headbands: Headbands were a popular accessory in the 2000s, and were often worn to hold back long hair or to add a touch of flair to an outfit.

8. Plastic jewelry: Plastic jewelry was a big trend in the 2000s, with many people opting for bright and colorful pieces.

9. Scrunchies: Scrunchies were another popular accessory in the 2000s, and were often worn to keep hair pulled back.

10. Oversized sunglasses: Oversized sunglasses were a must-have in the 2000s, and were often worn to protect eyes from the sun or to add a touch of glamor to an outfit.

5. Political events in the 2000s

In the 2000s, there were several significant political events that shaped the decade. One of the most notable was the rise of globalization, as countries around the world became increasingly interconnected through trade and commerce. This led to the formation of new international organizations such as the World Trade Organization (WTO) and the International Monetary Fund (IMF), which aimed to promote free trade and economic growth.

Another major event was the War on Terror, which began in response to the September 11th attacks in the United States. This led to increased military spending and the deployment of troops to various countries in the Middle East and beyond.

Additionally, there were several elections held during this time period that had a significant impact on politics. In the United States, the 2000 presidential election between George W. Bush and Al Gore was one of the closest in history, with Bush ultimately winning the presidency after a controversial recount in Florida. In the UK, Tony Blair's Labour Party remained in power throughout the decade, while in Canada, Paul Martin succeeded Jean Chretien as Prime Minister in 2003.

Overall, the 2000s saw a mix of both continuity and change in political landscape, with some countries experiencing political stability while others underwent significant shifts in leadership and policy.

6. Economic changes in the 2000s

The 2000s saw significant economic changes that had a profound impact on the world. One of the most notable changes was the rise of emerging markets such as China and India, which began to play a larger role in the global economy. This shift in power led to increased competition among developed countries and sparked debates about trade policies and protectionism. Additionally, the dot-com bubble burst in the early 2000s, leading to a recession that lasted until 2003. During this time, many companies went bankrupt and millions of people lost their jobs. However, the economy eventually recovered, and the stock market reached new highs in the latter half of the decade. Overall, the 2000s were marked by a period of economic growth and change, with implications that continue to shape the global economy today.

7. Social issues in the 2000s

The 2000s were a decade marked by significant social change. Issues such as race relations, gender equality, and LGBTQ+ rights came to the forefront of public discourse. The rise of social media platforms provided new ways for people to connect and organize around these issues, while also amplifying the voices of marginalized communities. At the same time, there were still many challenges facing society, including poverty, inequality, and discrimination. Despite progress being made, there was still much work to be done in the fight for a more equitable and just world.

8. The impact of the internet on society in the 2000s

The internet was a game changer in the 2000s, revolutionizing the way people connect and access information. It had a profound impact on society, transforming the way we communicate, work, learn, and even think. In the 2000s, the internet became an integral part of daily life, with billions of people around the world accessing it through their homes, schools, and offices. The internet provided new opportunities for communication, making it easier for people to stay connected with friends and family, no matter how far apart they were. It also made it easier for people to share their thoughts and ideas, creating a global community where people from all walks of life could exchange information and perspectives. However, the internet also brought its own set of challenges, including concerns over privacy, security, and the spread of misinformation. As the decade progressed, these issues became increasingly important, leading to debates and discussions about the role of the internet in society and the need for greater regulation. Despite these challenges, the internet continued to grow and evolve, with new technologies and innovations emerging that further transformed the way we live and work.

9. Advancements in science and medicine in the 2000s

The 2000s were a time of great advancement in science and medicine. From breakthroughs in genetic research to the development of new medical technologies, the decade saw some of the most significant achievements in these fields. One of the most notable developments was the mapping of the human genome, which paved the way for a better understanding of how our genes influence our health and disease. This led to the development of personalized medicine, where treatments are tailored to an individual's specific genetic makeup. Another major breakthrough was the creation of stem cells, which have the potential to become any type of cell in the body and can be used to treat a wide range of diseases. Additionally, there were significant advancements in the field of robotics, with robots being developed for use in surgery, manufacturing, and even space exploration. These advancements have greatly improved the quality of life for many people and hold great promise for the future of medicine.

10. Conclusion

In conclusion, the 2000s era was a time of great change and progress. From the rise of technology to the impact of the internet on society, there were many significant events and developments that shaped this decade. It was a time of growth and innovation, with new ideas and advancements emerging in various fields such as science and medicine. The 2000s era also brought about social changes, including the rise of new fashion trends and music genres. However, it was not without its challenges, as the decade also saw political upheaval and economic uncertainty. Overall, the 2000s era was a time of both progress and setbacks, and its impact can still be felt today.

Detroit Pistons: The Bad Boys of Basketball

1. Introduction to the Detroit Pistons

The Detroit Pistons are a professional basketball team based in Detroit, Michigan. They are members of the National Basketball Association (NBA) and began play in the 1945-1946 season. Over the years, the Pistons have had many successful seasons, including making it to the NBA Finals multiple times. However, one of the most iconic periods in their history was the "Bad Boys" era, which took place from the late 1970s to the early 1990s.

2. Origins of the "Bad Boys" nickname

The "Bad Boys" nickname originated in the late 1980s when the Detroit Pistons team became known for their physical play and aggressive defense. Led by players like Isiah Thomas, Joe Dumars, and Dennis Rodman, the Pistons consistently finished among the top teams in the league and made it to the NBA Finals three times between 1988 and 1991. Their tough, hard-nosed style of play earned them the moniker "Bad Boys," which has stuck with the franchise ever since.

3. Key players during the Bad Boys era

Several key players helped define the Detroit Pistons as the "Bad Boys" during their championship run in the late 1980s and early 1990s. Here are some of the most influential players from this era:

1. Isiah Thomas: Known for his aggressive playing style and leadership on the court, Thomas was one of the main architects of the Bad Boys'

success. He was a six-time All-Star and led the team in assists during the 1988-1989 season.

2. Joe Dumars: One of the greatest shooting guards in NBA history, Dumars was a clutch performer who played a key role in the Bad Boys' championship runs. He was a four-time All-Star and won three championships with the Pistons.

3. Dennis Rodman: "The Worm" was known for his defensive prowess and rebounding ability, as well as his eccentric personality off the court. He was a five-time All-Star and won two championships with the Pistons.

4. John Salley: A versatile forward who could score, rebound, and defend, Salley was a key player during the Bad Boys era. He was a three-time All-Star and won two championships with the Pistons.

5. Bill Laimbeer: A physical center who was notorious for his hard fouls and tough play, Laimbeer was a key contributor to the Pistons' championship runs. He was a four-time All-Star and won three championships with the team.

4. Coaching strategies during the Bad Boys era

During the Bad Boys era, the Detroit Pistons were known for their aggressive and physical play style, which was reflected in the coaching strategies employed by their head coach, Chuck Daly. Daly was known for his attention to detail and his ability to motivate his players to play with maximum effort and intensity. He emphasized the importance of teamwork and communication, and he implemented a number of different strategies to take advantage of the team's strengths while minimizing their weaknesses. One of the key aspects of Daly's coaching style was his use of the "zone defense," which allowed the Pistons to disrupt their opponents' offensive rhythm and force turnovers.

Additionally, Daly was known for his use of timeouts and his ability to communicate effectively with his players during games. Overall, Daly's coaching strategies played a significant role in the success of the Detroit Pistons during the Bad Boys era.

5. On-court tactics used by the Bad Boys

The Detroit Pistons' "Bad Boys" era was known for its aggressive and physical play style. The team's on-court tactics were designed to intimidate opponents and wear them down over the course of the game. Some of the key tactics used by the Bad Boys included:

* Full-court pressure defense: The Bad Boys would press their opponents from coast to coast, disrupting their offensive plays and forcing turnovers. This tactic helped to create fast break opportunities for the Pistons, who were known for their efficient scoring in transition.

* Physical play: The Bad Boys were not afraid to get physical with their opponents, using bumps and shoves to disrupt their movement and throw off their rhythm. This style of play earned the team its nickname, as they were seen as the "bad boys" of the league.

* Double teams: The Bad Boys often employed double teams on their opponents' best players, attempting to take them out of the game and force others to step up and score. This tactic helped to limit the production of opposing stars and keep the Pistons in control of the game.

* Trap defenses: The team would set traps in certain areas of the court, such as at the top of the key or in the post, in order to catch their opponents off guard and create turnovers.

Overall, the on-court tactics used by the Detroit Pistons during the Bad Boys era were designed to be unpredictable and disruptive, making it difficult for opponents to prepare for them.

6. Impact of the Bad Boys era on the NBA

The Detroit Pistons' "Bad Boys" era had a profound impact on the NBA, shaping the league in several ways. One of the most significant changes was the increased physicality and aggression on the court, which led to more intense and exciting games. The Bad Boys' tactics, such as their trademark "palm-up" defense and their willingness to foul opponents, made it clear that the team was not afraid to play rough. This style of play set a new standard for the league and inspired other teams to adopt similar strategies.

Another impact of the Bad Boys era was the increased attention on defense. Under coach Chuck Daly, the Pistons became known for their stifling defense, which often forced opponents into turnovers and fast break opportunities. This focus on defense helped to revolutionize the way the game was played, with many teams now prioritizing defensive strategies in order to compete at the highest level.

Additionally, the Bad Boys era helped to usher in a new era of superstar athletes. Players like Isiah Thomas, Joe Dumars, and Dennis Rodman were not only skilled on the court but also larger-than-life personalities who captivated fans with their charisma and swagger. These players helped to raise the profile of the NBA and attract a new generation of fans to the sport.

Finally, the Bad Boys era had a lasting impact on the culture of the NBA. The tough, physical style of play embodied by the Pistons inspired a new breed of fan who appreciated the intensity and intensity of the game. This style of play continues to be celebrated by fans to this day, and the legacy of the Bad Boys era lives on in the hearts of many.

7. Legacy of the Detroit Pistons as the "Bad Boys"

The Detroit Pistons' reign as the "Bad Boys" of basketball left an indelible mark on the league. Their aggressive playing style, physical defense, and fearless attitude on the court captivated fans and intimidated opponents. The team's success during this era inspired a generation of players to adopt similar tactics, leading to a shift in the way the game was played. The legacy of the Bad Boys can still be felt today, with many modern players citing them as an influence. Off the court, the team's tough-guy image and gritty mentality helped to redefine the culture of the NBA, paving the way for a new breed of athletes who were unafraid to push boundaries and challenge conventions. In this sense, the Detroit Pistons will always be remembered as the pioneers of the Bad Boys era, and their impact on the sport remains immeasurable.

8. Comparison to other dominant basketball teams

While the Detroit Pistons were undoubtedly one of the most dominant teams in NBA history during their "Bad Boys" era, they are not the only team to have achieved great success through tough, physical play. Other dominant basketball teams throughout NBA history include the Boston Celtics of the 1960s, who were known for their defensive prowess and ability to outmaneuver opponents; the Los Angeles Lakers of the 1980s, who dominated with their Showtime style of play; and the Golden State Warriors of recent years, who have consistently been one of the top teams in the league due to their versatile roster and innovative coaching strategies. However, each of these teams had their own unique approach to the game, and none can quite match the raw intensity and aggression that defined the Detroit Pistons' Bad Boys era.

9. Current state of the Detroit Pistons franchise

The current state of the Detroit Pistons franchise is one of rebuilding and growth. After a period of decline in performance and fan interest, the team has undergone significant changes in recent years. The front office has been revamped with new management and scouting staff, and the roster has seen several high draft picks and key acquisitions through trades.

Despite these efforts, the team remains in a rebuilding phase and is not currently competitive at the highest level of the NBA. However, there is hope for the future as the young talent on the roster continues to develop and the team's management continues to make smart decisions.

Overall, while the present state of the Detroit Pistons franchise may not live up to the glory days of the Bad Boys era, there is reason to believe that the team will eventually return to its former glory with continued hard work and dedication.

10. Conclusion: The enduring influence of the Bad Boys era

The conclusion of this article highlights the lasting impact of the Detroit Pistons' "Bad Boys" era on the NBA. Despite the team's decline in recent years, the legacy of the Bad Boys remains strong. Their aggressive playing style, physical defense, and toughness on the court have been emulated by many subsequent NBA teams. The Bad Boys era was a pivotal moment in NBA history, marking the beginning of a new era of competitive basketball. It set the stage for the next generation of players and teams, who sought to emulate their success and dominance on the court. The enduring influence of the Bad Boys era can still be felt in the NBA today, as teams continue to strive for the same level of intensity and toughness that defined the Bad Boys' reign.

The Detroit Pistons: A Look into Their Colorful History

1. Introduction to the Detroit Pistons

The Detroit Pistons are a professional basketball team based in Detroit, Michigan. They are members of the National Basketball Association (NBA) and began play in the 1945-1946 season. Over the years, the Pistons have had their fair share of ups and downs, but they have always remained a beloved and iconic part of the city of Detroit. In this article, we will take a look at the colorful history of the Detroit Pistons, from their early years to their recent successes and challenges.

2. Early Years of the Detroit Pistons

The early years of the Detroit Pistons were marked with a strong commitment to defense and physical play, which helped establish them as one of the top teams in the NBA during the 1950s and 1960s. Under the leadership of legendary coach Red Auerbach, the team made its first appearance in the NBA Finals in 1957, where they faced off against the Boston Celtics. Although they ultimately fell short in their quest for a championship, the Pistons remained competitive throughout the decade, highlighted by a run to the NBA Finals again in 1960. In the following years, the team struggled to find success on the court, but remained a beloved fixture in the Detroit community.

3. Pistons' Success in the 1980s

During the 1980s, the Detroit Pistons experienced unprecedented success on the court. Led by head coach Chuck Daly and a group of talented players including Isiah Thomas, Joe Dumars, and Dennis Rodman, the team became known as the "Bad Boys" due to their aggressive and physical playing style. In the 1987-88 season, the Pistons won an impressive 50 games and went all the way to the NBA Finals where they faced off against the Los Angeles Lakers. Despite losing the series, the Pistons had proven themselves as a force to be reckoned with in the league. Over the next few years, the team continued to dominate with five consecutive trips to the NBA Finals from 1988 to 1993.

4. The Bad Boys Era

During the late 1980s and early 1990s, the Detroit Pistons were known as the "Bad Boys." This era was marked by physical play, tough defense, and a fearless attitude on the court. Led by players like Isiah Thomas, Joe Dumars, and Dennis Rodman, the Pistons became one of the most dominant teams in the NBA during this time. They made it to the NBA Finals three times in a row from 1988 to 1991, winning back-to-back championships in 1989 and 1990. The Bad Boys Era was a testament to the power of teamwork, toughness, and determination. It remains a cherished part of Detroit Pistons history and a source of pride for fans of the team.

5. Challenges and Rebuilding Efforts

After experiencing success in the 1980s as one of the "Bad Boys" of the NBA, the Detroit Pistons faced several challenges in the following decades. Despite making the playoffs consistently during this time, they struggled to advance past the first round. In the early 2000s, the team was sold to new ownership, which began a period of rebuilding. The Pistons drafted young talent such as Darko Milicic and Rodney Stuckey, but these picks did not pan out as hoped. The team also made questionable trades, such as the acquisition of Ben Wallace from the Orlando Magic. Despite these setbacks, the Pistons were able to find some success in the late 2000s with the emergence of players like Chauncey Billups and Tayshaun Prince. However, the team continued to struggle in the playoffs, failing to advance past the second round. In recent years, the Pistons have undergone another rebuild, trading away key players such as Andre Drummond and Blake Griffin in an effort to restart their franchise.

6. Recent Years and Future Prospects

The Detroit Pistons have had their fair share of ups and downs over the years, and the past few seasons have been no exception. In recent years, the team has struggled to find consistent success on the court, with some lean seasons and high draft picks that failed to live up to expectations. However, despite these challenges, there is still reason to be optimistic about the future prospects of the Detroit Pistons.

One bright spot in recent years has been the emergence of young talent on the roster. Players like Luke Kennard, Bruce Brown Jr., and Sviatoslav Mykhailiuk have shown flashes of brilliance and have helped keep the team competitive even during tough times. Additionally, the team has made smart moves in the front office, bringing in experienced coaches and executives to guide the franchise back towards success.

Looking ahead to the future, the Detroit Pistons have a number of exciting prospects on the horizon. With another high draft pick this year, the team has the opportunity to add yet another talented player to their already impressive pool of young talent. Additionally, the team has a number of promising free agents set to hit the market, including star players like Blake Griffin and Andre Drummond, who could potentially re-sign with the team or bring in top talent from around the league.

Overall, while the past few years may not have been kind to the Detroit Pistons, there is still plenty of reason to be hopeful about the future. With a strong core of young players and smart management in place, the team is poised to make a comeback and return to its former glory as one of the most successful franchises in NBA history.

7. Key Players and Coaches

The Detroit Pistons have had many notable players and coaches throughout their history. In this section, we will take a closer look at some of the most influential figures in the team's success.

One of the most iconic players in Detroit Pistons history is Isiah Thomas. As a point guard, Thomas was instrumental in leading the team to its first championship in 1989. He was known for his speed, agility, and scoring ability, and was named the NBA Finals MVP that year. Thomas also played a key role in the Pistons' success during the Bad Boys era, using his leadership skills to guide the team through tough times.

Another important player in the team's history is Joe Dumars. As both a player and executive, Dumars played a crucial role in building the Pistons into a championship contender. As a shooting guard, he was a consistent scorer and helped lead the team to the NBA Finals in 1990. After retiring as a player, Dumars became the team's general manager and oversaw several successful draft picks, including Grant Hill and Chauncey Billups.

Other notable players who have donned the Pistons uniform include Dennis Rodman, Vince Ellis, and Bob Lanier. These players, along with others, helped shape the team's identity and made them a force to be reckoned with in the NBA.

In terms of coaching, the Detroit Pistons have had several successful coaches over the years. One of the most notable is Chuck Daly, who led the team to two NBA championships in the 1980s. Daly was known for his defensive strategies and his ability to motivate his players. Other notable coaches include Alvin Gentry, Larry Brown, and Stan Van Gundy.

8. Iconic Moments and Games

The Detroit Pistons have had many iconic moments and games throughout their history. Here are some of the most memorable ones:

1. "The Shot Heard 'Round the World": In 1980, with the score tied at 101, Isiah Thomas hit a buzzer-beating jumper to defeat the Houston

Rockets and advance the Pistons to the NBA Finals. This shot has been etched in the memories of Pistons fans ever since.

2. "The Malice at the Palace": On November 19, 2004, during a game against the Indiana Pacers, players from both teams got into a brawl on the court. The altercation resulted in several ejections and suspensions, and it remains one of the most infamous moments in NBA history.

3. "The Double-Double Dynasty": During the 1980s, center Bill Laimbeer and power forward Dennis Rodman led the Pistons to four straight NBA championships, with both players averaging double-doubles in points and rebounds.

4. "The 3-Point Revolution": In the early 2000s, the Pistons became known as the "Golden State Warriors of the East" due to their aggressive full-court press and fast-paced offense, which relied heavily on three-point shooting. They made the playoffs every year from 2000 to 2008, reaching the Eastern Conference Finals in 2008.

5. "The Return of the King": In 2016, after a brief retirement, Tim Duncan returned to the NBA as a coach for the Pistons. Although his tenure was short-lived, he brought a new level of professionalism and discipline to the team.

9. Fan Culture and Traditions

The Detroit Pistons have a passionate fan base known as "Piston Nation." These fans are known for their loyalty and dedication to the team, regardless of their success on the court. One of the most iconic traditions of Piston Nation is the "Victory Cigar," where fans celebrate a win with a cigar. This tradition has been passed down from generation to generation and is a symbol of the team's history and the unwavering support of its fans. Another popular tradition is the "Jalen Rose Garden Party," which takes place at Jalen Rose's home and brings together fans from all over the world to celebrate the team and its players. These traditions are just a few examples of the rich culture and history of the Detroit Pistons and their dedicated fan base.

10. Conclusion

The Detroit Pistons have a rich and colorful history that spans over 75 years. From their early days as a franchise to their current status as one of the most successful teams in NBA history, the Pistons have always been a team to watch. In this article, we have taken a look at some of the key moments and events that have shaped the Pistons' journey, from their early success in the 1980s to their challenges and rebuilding efforts in recent years. We have also explored the team's fan culture and traditions, and highlighted some of the key players and coaches who have helped to make the Pistons the team they are today. As the Pistons continue to move forward, it will be interesting to see what the future holds for this storied franchise.

Don't miss out!

Visit the website below and you can sign up to receive emails whenever Epic History publishes a new book. There's no charge and no obligation.

https://books2read.com/r/B-A-FTVBB-WSHYC

Did you love *Detroit Pistons Epic History*? Then you should read *Detroit Lions Fun Facts*[1] by Trivia Ape!

[2]

Discover the ultimate fan experience with the "Detroit Lions Fun Facts" book – an exciting journey through the rich history and legendary moments of this iconic NFL team. Packed with over 1000 detailed fun facts, this family-friendly book is designed to challenge and entertain fans of all ages while deepening their knowledge of the Detroit Lions.

Immerse yourself in the heart-pounding action, unforgettable plays, and standout players that have defined their legacy. From thrilling rivalries and historic divisional matchups to legendary offensive star players and iconic stadium facts, each question provides a captivating glimpse into the team's remarkable journey.

---

1. https://books2read.com/u/bW6QpG

2. https://books2read.com/u/bW6QpG

Unearth captivating insights into the team origins, relive iconic victories, and celebrate the achievements of Hall of Fame players who have graced the field for this epic franchise. With a careful balance of challenging facts and accessible content, readers will learn fascinating facts, engage in spirited discussions, and proudly display their Detroit Lions expertise.

Whether you're a lifelong fan looking to increase your knowledge or a newcomer eager to learn about their storied past, the "Detroit Lions Fun Facts" book is your go-to source for immersive entertainment.

Read more at www.triviaape.com.

Also by Epic History

New Jersey Devils Epic History
Detroit Red Wings Epic History
Dallas Mavericks Epic History
Denver Nuggets Epic History
Detroit Pistons Epic History
Golden State Warriors Epic History
Los Angeles Lakers Epic History